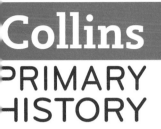

Collins
PRIMARY
HISTORY

Ancient Greece
Pupil Book

T0340507

Alf Wilkinson

William Collins' dream of knowledge for all began with the publication of his first book in 1819.
A self-educated mill worker, he not only enriched millions of lives, but also founded a flourishing publishing house.
Today, staying true to this spirit, Collins books are packed with inspiration, innovation and practical expertise. They place you at the centre of a world of possibility and give you exactly what you need to explore it.

Collins. Freedom to teach.

Published by Collins
An imprint of HarperCollins*Publishers*
The News Building
1 London Bridge Street
London
SE1 9GF

HarperCollins*Publishers*
Macken House, 39/40 Mayor Street Upper,
Dublin 1, DO1 C9W8, Ireland

Browse the complete Collins catalogue at
www.collins.co.uk

© HarperCollins*Publishers* Limited 2019
Maps © Collins Bartholomew 2019

10 9 8 7

ISBN 978-0-00-831084-4

British Library Cataloguing-in-Publication Data
A catalogue record for this publication is available from the British Library.

Author: Alf Wilkinson
Publisher: Lizzie Catford
Product developer: Natasha Paul
Copyeditor: Sally Clifford
Indexer: Jouve India Private Ltd
Proofreader: Nikky Twyman
Image researcher: Alison Prior
Map designer: Gordon MacGilp
Cover designer and illustrator: Steve Evans
Internal designer: EMC Design
Typesetter: Jouve India Private Ltd
Production controller: Rachel Weaver
Printed and bound by Martins the Printers

This book contains FSC™ certified paper
and other controlled sources to ensure
responsible forest management.

For more information visit:
www.harpercollins.co.uk/green

The publishers gratefully acknowledge the permission granted to reproduce the copyright material in this book. Every effort has been made to trace copyright holders and to obtain their permission for the use of copyright material. The publishers will gladly receive any information enabling them to rectify any error or omission at the first opportunity.

Contents

Jason and the quest for the Golden Fleece

'King Pelias ordered Jason to find the Golden **Fleece** and return with it to him. When news of Jason's voyage spread, people flocked to join his crew. Jason chose 50 of the strongest and bravest to go with him. They loaded the ship with food and jars of fresh water, and set off... Crowds on the shore cheered them off as they rowed away. At first the sea was rough and winds blew against the ship but then the Gods sent them a favourable wind and they were able to make good time... they had to pass through dangerous rocky waters and stormy seas. When they landed on islands for fresh food and water, they were often attacked by fierce people or monsters...'

Jason and his crew set sail on their ship, the Argo, to find the Golden Fleece.

What can we learn about the Ancient Greeks from the story of Jason and the Golden Fleece?

The mythical story of Jason and the Golden Fleece tells us a great deal about Ancient Greece. Jason's journey lasted many years and he faced many dangers both from people and from the gods. Jason successfully defeated all the challenges he faced with a mixture of cunning and bravery, and with help from the gods. He returned home with the Golden Fleece.

Steep hills and mountains cover much of Greece
▼

▲ Map of Ancient Greece

Barbarians were anyone who was not a Greek.

The Greeks loved stories, and we can still read many of them today. They were excellent sailors, and travelled far and wide around the Mediterranean. They spent a lot of their time fighting each other, as well as non-Greeks (who they called 'barbarians'). They also believed in many gods and made sacrifices to them to keep them happy.

Geography

Greece is in the Mediterranean. Its climate has warm wet winters and hot dry summers, making it good for growing crops. Vines, olives, wheat and vegetables grow quickly and easily. But much of the land is hilly, and in Ancient Greece it was used for grazing sheep and goats. However, some hillsides were **terraced**, to provide more farmland. Often, in Ancient Greece, the quickest way to travel was by sea. Greece is made up of around 6000 islands in total, and the coastline is 16,000 kilometres long! Fishing was a very important source of food.

Think about it!

1. How did the geography of Greece affect the Ancient Greeks' way of life?
2. Why do you think the sea was so important to the Greeks?

Key words

fleece
terraced
myth

Let's do it!

1. Read the rest of the story of Jason and his crew. What else can you learn about life in Ancient Greece from the **myth**?
2. Find out more about Mediterranean climates. How hot does it get in summer? How cool is it in winter? How would this affect farming?

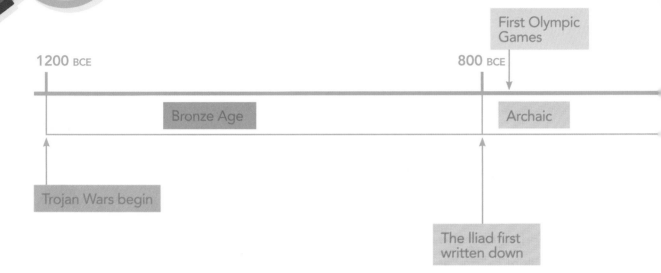

Defined by warfare

We can trace Greek culture back to the Mycenaeans in around 1550 BCE, but they disappear from history around 1200 BCE, the time of the Trojan Wars. Ancient Greece, as we think of it, appears around about 800 BCE. However, it is strongest in the 'Classical' period (around 450 BCE), after the defeat of the Persians in 480 BCE. Greece was united into one country by Philip of Macedonia and his son, Alexander the Great, who conquered the whole region and made it part of their empire in 338 BCE. When Alexander died, the empire fell apart and Greece was conquered by Rome in around 168 BCE. Greece did not appear on the map again as an independent country until the 1830s. This is when it won its independence from the **Ottoman Empire**, which was based in Constantinople.

As you can see, much of Greek history is defined by warfare! Most of this book focuses on the events in the Classical period of Ancient Greece, which is the period that has influenced us the most. Most of what we know about the people and achievements of Ancient Greece were 'lost' until the **Renaissance** in Europe. The Ancient Greeks became fashionable again, and people began to copy Greek ideas and buildings. It is important to be sure which period of Greek history you are talking about.

City-states

As you can see from the map on page 5, there were many different Greek cities, and each ran its own affairs. As with the Maya in Meso-America, a strong ruler might expand the size of the **city-state**, but a weaker ruler might be defeated and controlled by another. The two main city-states in Ancient Greece were Athens and Sparta, although there were many more.

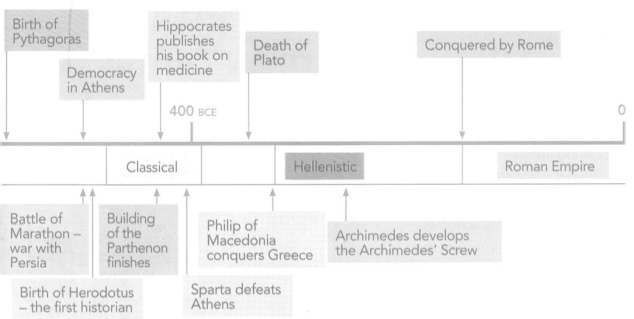

Birth of Pythagoras

Democracy in Athens

Hippocrates publishes his book on medicine

Death of Plato

Conquered by Rome

400 BCE

0

Classical

Hellenistic

Roman Empire

Battle of Marathon – war with Persia

Building of the Parthenon finishes

Philip of Macedonia conquers Greece

Archimedes develops the Archimedes' Screw

Birth of Herodotus – the first historian

Sparta defeats Athens

Athens

Athens was the biggest city in Ancient Greece, and had a population of 120,000 in 500 BCE. It was named after Athena, the goddess of wisdom and warfare. Democracy first appeared in Athens in 500 BCE. The area around Athens had good farmland. Also, the mountains had silver and lead mines and marble quarries, which helped to make the city very rich. Trade with other cities and countries was also important in making Athens rich and powerful.

Achilles killing the Amazon Queen Penthesilea, a jar ▶
*(**amphora**) made in Athens c530 BCE*

Think about it!

1. How might fighting so many wars affect the people of Ancient Greece?
2. What can we learn about the people of Athens from the amphora?

Let's do it!

1. Use the events on the timeline to make a list of some of the main achievements of the Ancient Greeks. Which do you think was the most important? Why? You will discover more about each of these as you work through this book.

2. Do some research, either in books or on the internet, to find out what made Athens so successful.

Key words

Ottoman Empire
Renaissance
city-state
amphora

At home with an Ancient Greek family

Many people were poor, making their living from farming. They often lived in simple houses made of sun-dried mud brick. Each house had small windows, without glass, as well as wooden shutters to keep out the sun and the heat. Most people didn't have bathrooms, and relied on streams or public baths for washing. Rich ladies would have a bath at home, as they had enough servants to carry water to fill the bath and empty it afterwards. Furniture was simple and usually made of wood, but rich people often had paintings on their walls and **mosaics** set into the floor. Lighting was provided by lamps filled with olive oil. However, these were smoky, so most people went to bed when it got dark and got up when the sun came up. Men and women often had separate parts of the house, and even ate separately.

Modern cutaway drawing of a Greek home

Slaves

Much of the hard work in Ancient Greece was carried out by slaves. Slaves worked in people's homes and on farms. Some slaves did very important work, acting as scribes or managers, but most were treated badly.

Food

The Greeks had a healthy diet, eating bread, cheese, fruit, vegetables and eggs. There was a lot of fish available – octopus was a favourite. Only the rich could afford meat, except on very special occasions. Bees were kept for honey, which was used to sweeten foods. Olive oil was used for cooking, cleaning and lighting. The main meal was in the evening, and big dinner parties were common. There might

Historians believe there were often as many slaves as free people in Ancient Athens.

be musicians and dancers for entertainment at these parties. Only men were allowed to attend them.

A visit to the market

Each town or village had a marketplace, or agora. This is where people would come to buy and sell their goods. Farmers from out of town would bring in their left over food and buy things they couldn't grow or make for themselves.

Fishmonger at work, from ▷ an Athenian pot

◁ *A visit to the agora*

Think about it!

1. Imagine you are visiting the agora in the picture. What can you see? Hear? Smell? What do you want to buy today? Can you find it for sale in the picture?
2. Why do you think many of the stalls have cloths above them?
3. What is going on in the middle of the marketplace? How can you tell?

Let's do it!

1. Find out about the fruit and vegetables Greeks grew and ate. In what ways were they different to what we grow and eat today?
2. Do you think the Greeks had a healthy diet?
3. Find out about the life of slaves in Ancient Greece.

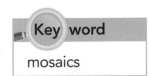

Key word

mosaics

What was life like for women in Ancient Greece?

Separate spheres

Women were very much under the control of their fathers, and then their husbands. Girls were usually married at the age of 13 or 14 – their father would decide who they were to marry. Girls didn't go to school, but their mothers would teach them how run a home. Girls in richer families might be taught to read and write like their brothers. Women were expected to look after the house. If they didn't have enough slaves, they might spend a lot of their time grinding grain into flour. They were taught to spin and weave, as this would bring in extra money to the household. Many women owned jewellery and bronze mirrors, and most used perfume. Poor women had to work, whereas rich women had more leisure time. Many men thought a woman's main job was to give birth to a son. Childbirth was dangerous and many women died giving birth.

Woman reading a scroll, from a vase c400 BCE

One of a woman's many chores was to fetch water from the public wells and fountains, as most houses didn't have their own water supply. Going shopping in the agora, or taking the slaves to do the shopping, also gave lots of women the chance to get out of the house. Many images show women talking with friends and neighbours while they collect water.

Think about it!

1. Do you think women were important in Ancient Greece?
2. In what ways were the lives of women in Ancient Greece different to the lives of women today?

Growing up in Ancient Greece

When a child was born, the mother handed it over to the father, and he decided whether to keep it or not. Some weak babies were left to die, while others were given away as slaves. From the age of 7, boys from wealthier families went to school. They were often accompanied by a slave, whose job it was to make sure they arrived at school safely. They were taught reading, writing and maths. They also learned to play a musical instrument, to learn and recite poetry by heart. When they were older, they learned to argue and debate. As future soldiers, they were also expected to be very fit – athletics, boxing and wrestling were very popular. Boys were regarded as adults when they were 12 or 13 years old and were expected to leave their childhood behind.

Boy being taught to write on a wax tablet using a wax scratcher or stylus

Many of the games children played might be familiar to us – knucklebones, spinning tops and board games were all popular. Dolls were common, and often made of rags, wood or pottery.

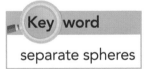

Key word

separate spheres

A children's toy

Let's do it!

1. Find out about the toys children played with, like the one in the picture above. How were they made? Did every Greek child have toys?
2. If you were growing up in Ancient Greece, would you rather have been a boy or a girl? Why?

Growing up in Sparta

As we saw in Unit 2.1, Sparta was one of the most important city-states of Ancient Greece. The Spartans were fierce warriors, and boys and girls were treated very much the same. They were expected to be supremely fit. From the age of 7, boys went to live in a barracks to train as soldiers. They didn't have enough food and were expected to steal food to survive. They were punished, not for stealing but for being caught. From the age of 20 until they were 60, men were expected to be soldiers. Even when they married, they lived in a barracks with their comrades, not with their wives. Spartan mothers sent their sons off to war with the words, 'Here is your shield, either come home with it or on it!'

Bowl from Sparta, c540 BCE

Working

There were three classes in Sparta. People born in Sparta were soldiers; immigrants worked as traders and craftsmen; and people captured in war became helots, or slaves. It was these helots who did all the work, and they were treated badly.

Women in Sparta

Helots, or slaves, did all the hard work in Sparta, including farming

Women had a much freer life in Sparta than in the rest of Greece, as their husbands were often away fighting or living in the barracks. They had more responsibility, and were able to come and go as they pleased. Gorgon, for example, born c518 BCE, was the daughter of the

King of Sparta, and she herself became Queen when he died. She was widely known as a wise and just ruler. Kyniska, born 440 BCE, was the first woman to win the four-horse chariot race at the Olympic Games (see Unit 6.3).

Interpretations

Unsurprisingly, historians disagree about the role of women in Ancient Greece. Some argue that they had few rights; others suggest they were much more important than we previously thought. And, of course, we have seen that things were very different in Sparta.

This is what one historian has to say about the role of women:

> 'Husbands expected wives to go out and those wealthy enough gave them slaves to accompany them... Indeed, one of the most important activities of women included visiting or helping friends and relatives. As men had their circle of friends, there is considerable evidence to indicate that women formed... friendships with neighbours, and visited one another frequently whether to borrow salt or a dress.'
>
> David Cohen, an American historian who studies Ancient Greece

Another historian writes:

> 'Free women were usually **secluded** so that they could not be seen by men who were not close relatives. An **orator** could maintain that some women were even too modest to be seen by men who were relatives.'
>
> Sarah Pomeroy, an American historian of Classical Greece who specialises in the history of women

Think about it!

1. How are these two views similar, and how are they different? Which one do you agree with? Why?
2. Which one matches the information in this unit best?

Let's do it!

1. Write your own interpretation of the role of women. Remember: you must have evidence to support your views.

Key words

secluded

orator

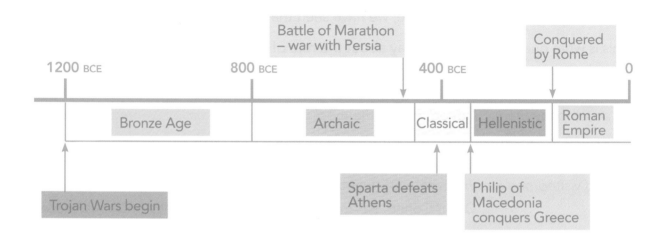

Battle of Marathon – war with Persia

Conquered by Rome

1200 BCE   800 BCE   400 BCE   0

| Bronze Age | Archaic | Classical | Hellenistic | Roman Empire |

Trojan Wars begin

Sparta defeats Athens

Philip of Macedonia conquers Greece

Each male citizen aged between 20 and 60 was expected to fight. They had to provide their own equipment. Weapons were a long wooden spear – 2.5 metres long with a bronze or iron tip – and a sword. Gleaming bronze armour would both protect the soldier and frighten the enemy. The large circular shield was around 80 centimetres in diameter, and made of wood, leather and bronze. Altogether this equipment weighed 20 kilograms.

A modern drawing of a Greek soldier, or hoplite

Soldiers would form a **phalanx**, or shield wall, and stand close together with their shields overlapping for protection. The bravest and most experienced soldiers were in the front row. Armies would come together in a kind of pushing contest. They would use their swords and spears and try to break ranks and force the enemy to flee. Discipline was the key to success, which explains all the hours spent training.

Think about it!

1. Imagine what it would be like being in the front row of the **phalanx**. Jot down your ideas and thoughts.
2. If you were attacking a Greek army, where would be the best place to attack? Why?

The Wooden Horse and Troy

The Greeks had been fighting the city of Troy for 10 years with little success. Finally, they built a wooden horse and left it outside the city walls and pretended to sail away. The Trojans (people of Troy) pulled the horse inside the walls. They didn't know that the horse was full of Greek soldiers, who emerged at night and opened the city gates. This allowed the whole Greek army into the city, which they then destroyed.

War against the Persians

In 490 BCE, the Persians invaded Greece. They used 600 ships to bring over 20,000 soldiers and cavalry. The Greeks had around 10,000 **hoplites**. The armies drew up on a plain near Marathon, 26 miles (42 kilometres) from Athens. Surprisingly, a brave attack by the Greeks killed nearly 7,000 Persians and forced them to flee. Philippides, a messenger, ran all the way from Marathon to Athens (without stopping) to bring the good news. This was the origin of the modern-day marathon race. At the Battle of Thermopylae in 480 BCE, a tiny force of Spartans, led by King Leonidas, bravely held up a huge force of Persians. But then Athens was destroyed.

Modern-day statue celebrating Philippides' run from Marathon to Athens in 490 BCE
▼

Let's do it!

1. Research one of the wars mentioned here. Who was fighting? Why? What were the main events? Who won, and what were the consequences for the Ancient Greeks?
2. Do you think the Greeks were clever fighters?

Key words

phalanx

hoplites

Trireme

Look carefully at the photograph of the modern-day replica **trireme**. Can you figure out how it works? Why do you think it is called a trireme?

Modern replica of an Ancient Greek trireme

The Greeks 'borrowed' the idea of triremes from the **Phoenicians** in around 700 BCE. The wealth of Athens let them build a huge fleet of warships. Each one was about 37 metres long, and 6 metres wide, weighing about 50 tonnes. It was lightweight, so it could easily be lifted out of the water, to prevent the wood from rotting. Two sails provided power on windy days, but the main power came from the three rows of oars on each side of the ship – nearly 180 rowers in total – giving a top speed of around 10 **knots** (19 kilometres per hour) over short distances. As well as being fast, they were very easy to move – they could turn around completely in less than 100 metres! The triremes were safest in calm waters, so battles were nearly

The Battle of Salamis, 480 BCE – during the war against the Persians

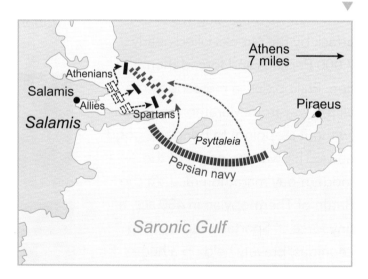

always fought near land. Before battle, all unnecessary weight (including the sails) was dumped ashore. Unusually, all the rowers **volunteered** for the job. They were not slaves, as in Ancient Egypt and Ancient Rome.

The Battle of Salamis – the greatest sea battle in the Ancient World?

As we have already discovered, the Greeks were defeated at Thermopylae in 480 BCE, despite the bravery of the Spartans under King Leonidas. The Persians then attacked and burned down the city of Athens, even destroying the **Parthenon**. The Greek navy retreated to Salamis, where they forced the Persian navy to fight in the narrow sea between Salamis and Piraeus. More than 800 Persian ships faced the 370 Greek triremes. Because of the narrow **strait**, the Persians could not attack the Greeks with all their ships. The leading Persian ships were trapped between the Greeks and the rest of their own ships. The Greeks struck them, using the bronze rams fixed to the front of their triremes. They sank over 300 Persian ships. Hoplites then boarded the Persian ships, killing the enemy. Thousands of Persian soldiers and sailors died, which forced the rest of the navy to flee. Athens was safe. Persia never attacked Greece again. The defeat of the Persians led to the start of the Classical period in Greece.

Athens v Sparta

It was probably unavoidable that the two key city-states would fight each other. The Peloponnesian Wars lasted from 431 BCE to 404 BCE, when Sparta defeated Athens. This brought the Classical age of Ancient Greece to an end. The Spartans were so impressed with the bravery of the Athenian soldiers that they did not destroy the city of Athens.

Dish showing fighting in the Peloponnesian Wars

Think about it!

1. What do you think it would be like fighting on an Athenian trireme?
2. In what ways would it be different to fighting on land?
3. Why do you think all the rowers were volunteers?

Let's do it!

1. Research the replica trireme called the *Olympias*. What have historians found out about the Ancient Greek navy from the replica?
2. Do you think the *Olympias* has been a success?
3. Research other ancient naval sea battles. Compare them to Salamis. Write a brief report called 'Ancient sea battles'.

Key words

trireme
Phoenicians
knots
volunteered
Parthenon
strait

There is plenty of evidence about Greek wars. We have already come across pictures of fighting on pottery.

Myths and poems

The story of the Wooden Horse and Troy first appears in the poem the *Odyssey*, written by Homer in the 8th century BCE. However, many people believe that the story had been told for hundreds of years before that.

*'But come now, change thy theme, and sing of the building of the horse of wood, which Epeius made with Athena's help, the horse which once Odysseus led up into the **citadel** as a thing of guile, when he had filled it with the men who **sacked** Troy.'*

Herodotus, the first historian, born 484 BCE

Herodotus went to live in Athens around 450 BCE and he wrote an account of the wars with Persia and the battles of Marathon and Thermopylae. He used eyewitness accounts of events, as well as his own knowledge and stories told about the events he was writing about. He was the first person to put together a convincing **historical narrative** of events that involved Athens and the Greek world.

Artefacts

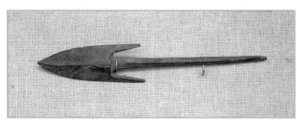

Bronze arrowhead from 4th-century-BCE Greece

Bronze helmet from Corinth, on show in a museum in Munich, Germany

A Spartan sword, made of iron, perhaps 30–45 centimetres long

Think about it!

1. In your opinion, which of these types of evidence is most useful in telling us about warfare in Ancient Greece?

How important was war to the Ancient Greeks?

We have already seen how warlike the Spartans were. Their whole society was based around war. Boys trained to be soldiers from the age of 7, and were expected to fight if needed until they were 60. Nothing brought greater honour than being killed in battle. Other cities, like Athens, also expected their citizens to equip themselves, to train and to fight.

There are lots of different kinds of evidence in history. Some is more useful than others.

If you look at the timeline on page 14, you can see that there were wars throughout the history of Ancient Greece. There were wars to fight off invaders, like the Persians, and to protect their city; wars to expand their city and make it richer and/or more important, like the Trojan Wars; and wars between city-states, like the battles between Sparta and Athens. It was also war – defeat by the Macedonians of Philip and Alexander the Great, and then by the Romans – that led to the end of Greece as an independent country.

Let's do it!

1. Look back carefully at all the evidence about warfare in Ancient Greece in this unit.
2. Select the evidence that suggests war *was* very important to the Ancient Greeks. Make a list of all the evidence supporting this idea.
3. Can you find any evidence that argues that war was *not* important to them? Make a list of that evidence.
4. Which list is longer? Which has stronger evidence?
5. Now use both your lists to help you answer this question: 'How important was war to the Ancient Greeks?'
6. Present your answer to the rest of your class.

Key words

citadel
sacked
historical narrative

Religion was very important to the Ancient Greeks. They thought the gods were like humans – sometimes happy, sometimes sad; sometimes helpful, sometimes disruptive. It was very important that the gods were kept happy, or they would make life for humans very bad indeed.

Mount Olympus, the highest mountain in Greece, was thought to be home of the gods

Household gods

Every home would have a small altar or **niche** for prayer. It might be outside in the courtyard, if the house was big enough, or it might be inside. At the entrance to the house there would also be **shrines** to the 'doorway gods', and it was their job to protect everybody and everything inside the house. Regular gifts, however small, would be made to these gods, to keep them happy.

City gods

Each city or town would have its own god, special to that place. Athena, for example, was the goddess for Athens. She gave olive trees to the Greeks, making them rich. Her special symbol was an owl, and pictures of owls often appeared on coins made in Athens. To make sure Athens remained safe and healthy, there were temples to her in the city, and special ceremonies to keep her happy. This temple was built in 431–429 BCE – while Athens was at war with Sparta – to help guarantee victory for Athens. As we already know, Sparta beat Athens, so building a temple didn't work in this case!

Zeus and his friends

There were many gods to keep happy. Zeus was the king of the gods. He was married to Hera. They had lots of children, and each one was god of a

Temple to Athena, in Athens

different aspect of life. Some gods were not related to Zeus, but they still called him 'Father'. Poseidon was the god of the sea, Aphrodite was the goddess of love and Artemis was the god of hunting. Demeter was the goddess of farming; and Apollo, the god of healing and medicine. Hades was the only god not to live on Mount Olympus – he was the god of the Underworld. As you can see, whatever you were planning or hoping to do, there was a god who could help or get in your way.

A sculpture of Zeus

Think about it!

1. Do you think religion was very important to the Ancient Greeks?

Let's do it!

1. Make a list of all the Greek gods and goddesses you can discover. Write down what they were associated with.
2. Choose one god or goddess and find out all you can about them. Make a presentation to your class about 'your' Greek god/goddess.
3. Write a diary for a day. Beside each activity you do, write the name of the Greek god/goddess you might have had to pray to for their help if you were an ancient Greek.

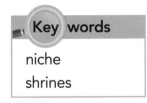

Key words

niche

shrines

No Ancient Greek would ever make a big decision in their life without consulting either a **soothsayer** or an oracle. They were thought to be able to look into the future and provide clear guidance on what to do. Soothsayers and oracles were said to be the voices of the gods. Probably the most famous oracle in the whole Greek world was at the temple of Apollo, at Delphi, built high up on Mount Parnassus. People came from all over the world to consult the Oracle of Delphi.

The Oracle of Delphi as it is today

Visiting the Oracle

People rich and poor would come and make sacrifices to the Oracle and ask for help in deciding what to do. Croesus was King of Lydia (part of modern Turkey, see map) and one of the richest people in the world at the time. He consulted the Oracle of Delphi before attacking Persia. The Oracle told him, 'If you cross the river, a great empire will be destroyed'. Croesus thought this meant he would defeat Persia. However, what happened was that he lost, and a great empire – his own – was destroyed.

It wasn't just rich people and rulers who came to Delphi. Ordinary people came too. Sometimes, lead tablets with questions written on them were handed to the Oracle. Two have been discovered. Heracleidas, for example, asked if his wife would give him children. Cleotas asked if keeping sheep was a good business to get into. These were important questions for ordinary people. Unfortunately, we don't know the answers they were given!

Map showing location of Lydia

The Oracle listened to the questions, then drank water from the sacred spring inside the temple. She prayed for guidance and then chanted her answers. Her helpers would write the answers down and then pass them on.

Every month, people would come and offer sacrifices to the Oracle. It might be a goat or a bull. They would then wait until the Oracle gave them an answer. If they were pleased with the answer, they might leave gifts at the temple, such as gold, silver, precious cups and bowls. Delphi became very rich! Often, as in the case of King Croesus, the reply might be quite vague, so the person asking the question had to decide for themselves what to do. Perhaps, that way, the Oracle could never be wrong.

◀ *A family sacrifice a goat as an offering*

Think about it!

1. What do you do when you have to make an important decision? Who do you ask for advice?
2. Does visiting the Oracle prove that Greeks were very religious?

Let's do it!

1. Who could become a priestess in Ancient Greece? How important were they?
2. Find out more about Ancient Greek soothsayers and oracles. Were there others as important as the one at Delphi?
3. What other sacrifices did Ancient Greeks make to the gods?

Key word

soothsayer

The Greeks loved stories and myths. Some involved the gods, but many involved heroes such as Herakles and Icarus. Many had a moral.

The Twelve Labours of Herakles

In a fit of madness, Herakles killed his wife and children. As punishment, he was told to serve King Eurystheus for 12 years. He was given 12 labours to carry out, and each one was thought to be impossible. They involved fighting mythical beasts and angry gods, and carrying out acts of great strength. Despite everything, Herakles survived and became a great hero – perhaps the greatest hero in Greek mythology.

"UP THEY ROSE, THE BOY AFTER HIS FATHER"

Painting showing the myth of Daedalus and Icarus

◀ *Greek stamp showing Herakles using a sling to kill the Stymphalian birds*

Aesop's fables

Aesop is thought to have been a slave. He was probably born in Ethiopia, and lived in Athens around 600 BCE. His stories were used both to entertain and to educate. It was originally thought all the tales were made up by Aesop, but some have been found in Ancient Egypt. Therefore, it is more likely that he collected tales, as well as wrote them.

Aesop's fables are still widely read today!

This fable is typical of Aesop:

A Fox was boasting to a Cat of its clever ways for escaping its enemies. "I have a whole bag of tricks," he said, "which contains a hundred ways of escaping my enemies." "I have only one," said the Cat; "but I can generally manage with that." Just at that moment they heard the cry of a pack of hounds coming towards them, and the Cat immediately scampered up a tree and hid herself. "This is my plan," said the Cat. "What are you going to do?" The Fox thought first of one way, then of another, and while he was deciding the hounds came nearer and nearer, and at last the Fox in his confusion was caught up by the hounds and soon killed by the huntsmen.

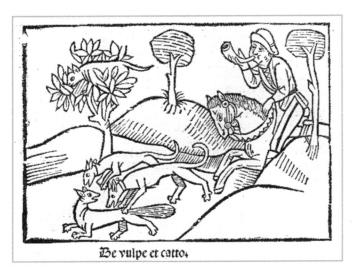

◀ *Illustration of the fable 'The Fox and the Cat', by Heinrich Steinhöwel, 1501*

Think about it!

1. What do you think is the moral of this fable?
2. Why might fables like this be attractive to Ancient Greeks?

Let's do it!

1. Find out about the myth of Daedalus and Icarus. How similar is this story to Aesop's 'The Fox and the Cat'?
2. At the start of this unit we stated that religion was very important to the Ancient Greeks. You should now be able to decide this for yourself.
3. Decide the best way to present your work on Greek religion. It might be written, a poster or a PowerPoint presentation. Make sure you use plenty of evidence to support your ideas. Have fun!

Where did the Greeks have colonies?

Greek cities and colonies around the Mediterranean Sea, coloured in dark green

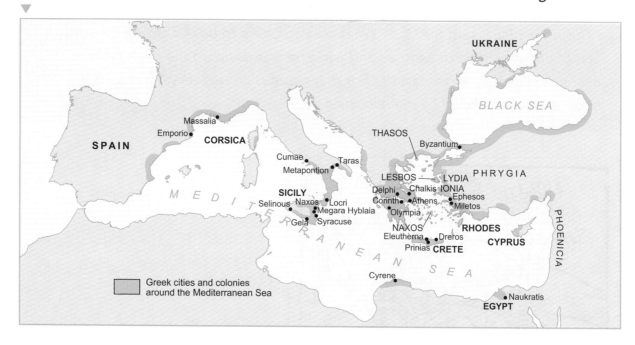

Between 800 BCE and 400 BCE, the Greek population grew rapidly. Some historians think it grew from 800,000 people in 800 BCE to around 10 million in 400 BCE. All these extra people needed food and clothing. There just wasn't enough good farmland in Greece for everybody, so more and more people went to sea – some to trade and some to find somewhere to live.

Some colonies, like Naucratis on the River Nile, were set up to connect with trade from more distant regions. Others were military cities, set up to protect trade routes.

Wealth and influence

As you can see from the map, Greek sailors never strayed very far from land. They didn't have a compass, and had to rely on the stars for navigation. New Greek cities and colonies grew up all around the Mediterranean and Black Sea coasts.

A Greek silver coin, c400 BCE

By 500 BCE, it was thought that around 40 per cent of all Greeks lived in one of these 500 colonies or cities dotted around the Mediterranean area. Some of these colonies became very wealthy. For example, Sybaris, in southern Italy, which was founded in 720 BCE, was so rich that its inhabitants were said to go to sleep each night on a bed of rose petals! There were so many Greeks living in southern Italy and Sicily that the area became known as Magna Graecia, or 'Greater Greece'.

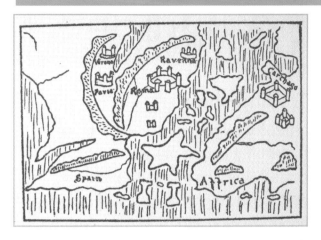

An Anglo Saxon map from the 10th century showing the Pillars of Herakles separating Spain from Africa

These colonies were wealthy enough to make their own coins, and they were expected to send troops and ships to fight in the various Greek wars.

Think about it!

1. Look carefully at the map of Greek colonies. What do you notice about the location of these colonies?
2. Do you think the growth of these colonies was caused by 'push' factors – people forced out of Greece – or 'pull' factors – the attraction and wealth of these new places?
3. Why do you think there is an image of a chariot pulled by four horses on the coin?

Pillars of Herakles

According to ancient myth, the gap separating North Africa and Gibraltar was created by Herakles on his tenth labour, which was to bring back the cattle of King Geryon (see Unit 4.3). He is said to have split the mountains in half with his sword. Very few Ancient Greeks dared to sail out from the Mediterranean into the Atlantic. As far as the Ancient Greeks were concerned, the Pillars of Herakles were, in effect, the end of the world!

Let's do it!

1. Research some of the Greek colonies. When were they set up? What made them wealthy?
2. Was having colonies around the Mediterranean Sea a good thing for the Ancient Greeks?

27

Trading ships

In 1968 the wreck of a Greek ship was found off the coast of Cyprus. It has been carefully preserved, and a replica was built to help archaeologists find out more about shipping and trade. The **Kyrenia,** as it is known, would have needed a crew of only four sailors and would have carried a cargo of around 400 amphorae. Archaeologists think it is typical of many smaller boats that traded around the coastal ports of the Mediterranean Sea at that time. They were very short and wide, with a shallow **draught**, which allowed them to land on a beach if necessary.

An engraving showing a boat similar to the Kyrenia, *a Greek merchant ship from around 300* BCE

Steering oars at the rear kept the ship on course, and there would be oars to move the ship in a harbour, for example. They could travel at around 5 knots (about 9 kilometres per hour), depending on the strength of the wind. It must have been quite a lonely existence spending weeks on end aboard ship as you sailed from port to port picking up and dropping off cargoes.

An amphora showing olive harvesting

Imports and exports

Most imports were foods and luxury goods. Fish, wheat, meat and timber were imported in huge quantities. Papyrus from Egypt was used for writing. Tin from Britain, gold from Egypt and copper from Cyprus were also imported. Other imports were more luxurious – spices and pearls from India and Afghanistan, silks from China, dyes from the Middle East, ivory from Africa, and apples and figs too. Perhaps the biggest import of all was slaves, as the whole Greek way of life depended on having huge quantities of slaves.

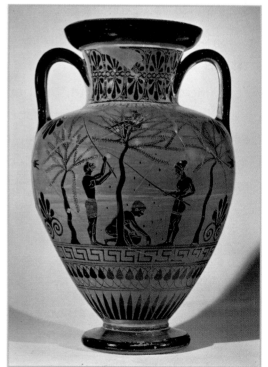

Exports were mostly olive oil, honey, pottery and metalwork of all kinds. Greek pottery was in particular demand throughout the region. Goods like oil and honey were exported in amphorae – huge jars that are found in great quantities amongst shipwrecks throughout the Mediterranean.

Recent research using **DNA** has found **residue** of several different substances – including nuts, vegetables and herbs – inside amphorae. This suggests they were recycled by sailors and used many times, and not just used to transport liquids.

Amphorae come in all shapes and sizes. It used to be thought they were only used once.

◀ *Amphorae stacked in a boat*

Think about it!

1. What would it be like to be part of the crew of a ship like the *Kyrenia*?
2. In what ways is the *Kyrenia* similar to, and different from, a trireme (see Unit 3.2)?
3. Why do you think the amphorae were that shape?

Key words

draught
DNA
residue

Let's do it!

1. Make *either* a trade map *or* an import–export grid for Ancient Greece. What does your work tell us about the Greeks?
2. In your opinion, why did the Greeks spread right across the known world? Was it necessity – shortage of land, for example – or was it a need for adventure? Can you think of any more causes? Make a list. Which of your causes do you think is the most important? Why?

Pytheas was born in Massalia (modern-day Marseilles, France) in 350 BCE. Massalia was a Greek colony. It was founded in 600 BCE as a means of controlling trade in the Western Mediterranean. Pytheas is perhaps the first true geographer, although he has also been described as a merchant and an explorer. His book, *On the Ocean* published in 320 BCE, made him famous throughout the Greek world, but many people at the time thought he had made it all up! Only a few short extracts from his book remain today.

Modern statue of Pytheas in Marseilles, France

The voyage

In 325 BCE, Pytheas set out on a major voyage of discovery. He may well have been the first Greek to sail beyond the Pillars of Herakles, out of the known world and into the unknown. He may have sailed into the Atlantic around Spain and along the French coastline. However, some historians argue that the first part of his journey was by land, across the South of France, to the mouth of either the River Loire or the Garonne. From there, he travelled by boat to Brittany, describing and measuring the coast as he went. From Brittany, he crossed to Cornwall, to find out where tin came from. He described a tin mine and the way tin was extracted, then sent to France and the Mediterranean.

The 'Congealed Sea' – 'pancake ice' near Sweden

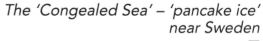

Next he explored the coasts of Wales and Scotland. He then headed (via the Hebrides, Orkneys and Shetland Isles) to Iceland, which he visited long before the Vikings did. Here he discovered what he called the 'Congealed Sea'. Presumably, he had reached the Arctic, where the sea was frozen. He also described the land of the midnight sun – something no one from the

Mediterranean world had seen before. This is where daylight lasted for 24 hours at the height of summer.

Pytheas sailed around Britain – as far as we know, he was the first person to do so. Then he explored the Baltic coast of Europe, searching for the source of amber, another product in great demand in the Mediterranean. Finally, after **circumnavigating** Britain, Pytheas headed for home, where he wrote down his experiences. He was the first man to measure accurately both the size and shape of Britain, and also to work out its **latitude** using the height of the sun. He knew exactly how far north of Massalia he had travelled.

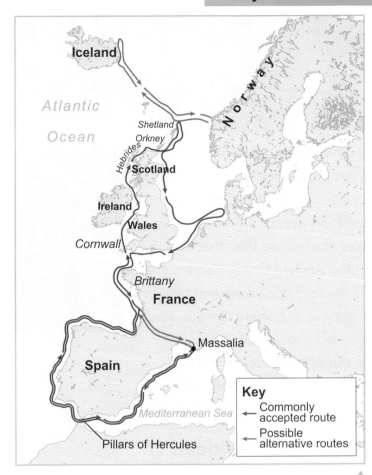

The voyage of Pytheas c325 BCE

Think about it!

1. Does the statue give an accurate view of Pytheas?
2. How brave do you think Pytheas was?
3. Many people at the time thought Pytheas had made up all the stories in his book. Why do you think this is?

Let's do it!

1. What does studying the voyage of Pytheas add to our knowledge of the Ancient Greek world?
2. Do you agree that, in fact, Pytheas was the first geographer? What else do you need to know to be able to answer this?
3. Pytheas died in 285 BCE. Write his **obituary**.

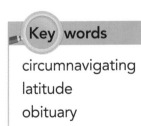

Key words

circumnavigating

latitude

obituary

Everyone has heard of the Olympic Games, where people come together to take part in sporting events. However, there was much more than that involved in the Ancient Greek Games. The Olympic Games were first held in Olympia, in Ancient Greece. Any free-born man, from anywhere in the whole Greek Empire, had a right to compete in the Games. Winning would make him famous.

Chariot racing shown on a Greek vase

Honouring the dead

It is thought that the very first Greek Games were held to honour soldiers killed in battle. In Homer's *The Iliad*, Achilles ordered a series of contests for his friend Patroclus, who had been killed during the Trojan Wars. After the Games, which began with chariot racing, they held a huge feast to remember the dead hero.

Running, as shown on an Athenian vase

Honouring the gods

Greeks thought that one of the best ways to honour their gods was to be very fit. To them, it was logical that the Games were held in sacred places, as they hoped the Games would keep the gods happy. There were Games in Athens, in honour of Athena; in Delphi, to honour Apollo; and at Corinth. However, the most famous Games were at Olympia, in honour of Zeus, King of the gods. Men arriving at the Games were expected to make gifts to the gods, and swear to obey the rules in front of the altar in the temple.

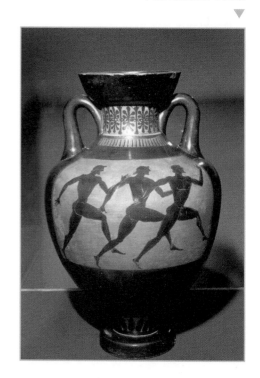

Having fun

The Games were a great social event too. People would meet up, catch up on all the news and gossip, or have a party. At the Olympic Games, for example, 100 cows were **sacrificed** at the start of the Games. Then they made offerings to Zeus, and the rest of the meat was shared out among everyone who was there. As ordinary Greeks rarely ate meat, this was a special occasion! Games were so popular that sometimes 20,000 men were there. Women were not allowed to compete in the Games.

A Greek amphora showing jumping. The athlete is holding iron or stone weights in each hand to help him jump further

Training for war

The Games had a much more serious role too. They were seen as an ideal way to prepare young men for war. War was almost a way of life, as the Greek city-states were often fighting each other. Many of the events required great fitness and developed the skills that hoplites needed in order to fight effectively. Good soldiers needed discipline, fitness and courage. It was thought that these qualities were best developed by sport.

Think about it!

1. Which was the most important reason for the Greeks holding the Games?
2. Why do you think people went to watch the Games?

Let's do it!

1. Find out more about the funeral Games that Achilles held for Patroclus. Which other events did the Athenian soldiers compete in? What were the prizes?
2. Why do you think women were banned from the Games?
3. In your opinion, were the Games fun or hard work?

Key word

sacrificed

The Olympic Games

By far the most famous games were the Olympic Games. They were first held in 776 BCE, and were held every four years without a break until 393 CE, when they were banned by the Romans. In 1896, they were revived in Athens, in an attempt to promote friendship and cooperation between countries. Wars stopped for a month around the times of the Games, to allow athletes to get to Olympia. On one occasion, the Spartans were banned from competing in the Games – for refusing to stop fighting!

Statue of a discus thrower. This is a Roman copy of a Greek bronze statue

Think about it!

1. Why might the Romans ban the Olympics in 393 CE?

Which events were part of the Olympics?

To begin with, the main event was the running race. This was just one length of the Olympic stadium. Winners were given a laurel wreath. They would also receive free meals for life from their home city, and statues were erected to remind people of their victory. Over time, more and more events were added. You can see some of these in Unit 6.1. The Games just got bigger and bigger!

Cheating!

Despite the threat of shame and flogging if they were discovered, some athletes did try to cheat. Some people bribed judges, or offered money to other athletes to lose their event. Others even wrote 'curse-tablets' – messages inscribed on lead and presented to the gods – in an attempt to gain an unfair advantage. Whatever the good intentions of the Games' organisers, there were always some people who wanted to bend the rules.

Wrestling was one of the first sports introduced at the Olympic Games

Continuity and change – the Ancient Olympics

Historians are very interested in how things change, and what this can tell us about the past. For instance, which new events were added to the Games, and why was this? Did the Games last longer? Did more people attend them? Did more athletes take part in the Games? Did they remain as important throughout the whole period of Ancient Greece as they were in 776 BCE?

Javelin throwing

Continuity and change – the modern Olympics

Today, the Olympic Games are still held every four years. People travel from all around the world to take part in the Games – both the Winter and Summer Olympics. There are also Paralympic Games for disabled athletes. Millions of people watch the events on television.

Let's do it!

1. Find out which sports were added to the Ancient Olympics over time.
2. How much continuity, and how much change, was there over the whole period of the Ancient Olympics?
3. How similar are the modern Olympics to the Ancient Greek Games? What has stayed the same? What has changed?
4. Do you think the modern Olympics have the same aims, ideas and values as the Ancient Greek Games?

No one is sure whether young unmarried women were allowed to watch the Olympics. Some historians say they were – in order to help them find a suitable husband. Married women were definitely banned, and no woman was allowed to take part in events.

Pausanias, who died in 180 CE, tells the story of one woman, Callipateira, who did attend the Olympic Games, so she could watch her son take part in the boxing:

> 'She disguised herself exactly like a gymnastic trainer, and brought her son to compete at Olympia. Her son was victorious, and Callipateira, as she was jumping over the enclosure in which they keep the trainers shut up, bared her person. So her sex was discovered, but they let her go unpunished out of respect for her father, her brothers and her son, all of whom had been victorious at Olympia. But a law was passed that for the future trainers should strip before entering the arena.'

Why did Callipateira have to disguise herself as a man to watch her son compete in the Olympics?

Statue of a woman athlete, now in the National Archaeological Museum, Athens

Kyniska of Sparta – the first female winner of an event in the Olympics

Kyniska, a Spartan woman, was born around 440 BCE. She was the daughter of the King. She won the four-horse chariot race, not once but twice – in 396 BCE and 392 BCE. She couldn't actually drive the chariot herself in the race, but the winner was the owner of the team (not the drivers, who were often slaves). A bronze statue of her, her horses and chariot was erected at Olympia.

The Games of Heraea

Around 600 BCE, women were allowed their own Games. These were in honour of the goddess Hera, who was the wife of Zeus. They were held in the Olympic stadium before the Olympic Games. Married women were unable to compete. These Games only included foot races, which were run over the Olympic course, but had a shorter distance. There were separate races for girls, maidens and young women. Athletes wore their hair loose, a simple **chiton** that came down to around the knee. The Games of Heraea were very important. Winners received a crown of olive leaves – just like the men – and were praised throughout the area. Their portraits were pinned on the columns of the Temple of Hera so everyone could see them.

Amphora from around 490 BCE showing Nike, the goddess of victory. Amphorae like this were often presented to the winners of races

Think about it!

1. How similar were the Games of Heraea to the Olympics?
2. Why do you think Callipateira wanted to watch the Olympics? And why was she not punished for breaking the rules?

Let's do it!

1. Kyniska was from Sparta. We know Spartan women were different to women in the rest of Ancient Greece. Find out more about her life.
2. Why were Games for women introduced in around 600 BCE?
3. We discovered in Unit 2 that the life of Greek women was very different to the life of Greek men. Has anything you have discovered on this page changed that view?

Key word

chiton

Who was the most important Ancient Greek?

Famous Ancient Greeks

We have already come across Homer, who wrote The *Iliad*, the epic poem of the Trojan Wars (or perhaps he was the first to write it down). We have also met Herodotus and his book about the wars with Persia. Herodotus is regarded as the first historian. He used all the sources he could find, interviewed eye witnesses, and wrote what he saw to be the truth about the wars. We have also discovered Pytheas, who many claim was the first geographer. On his voyage, he noted latitude, mapped the coastline of Britain, and described natural features of the Arctic, such as the 24-hour daylight and frozen sea. His book was the first book to talk about travel. He did not just give handy hints on how to get to your destination; he really was an explorer.

A sculpture of Herodotus in Athens

At the theatre

Greeks loved going to the theatre. Sometimes they went to listen to poetry competitions, but more often they went to see the plays. Theatres were huge, semicircular buildings and were always open-air. The actors were all men, who wore masks to represent the characters they were playing. Early plays had just one actor playing all the parts, but later there were more. There was also a chorus who described and commented on the main action of a play with songs and dance. If the audience

Remains of the Greek theatre at Epidaurus, built in the 4th century BCE. It held about 12,000 spectators

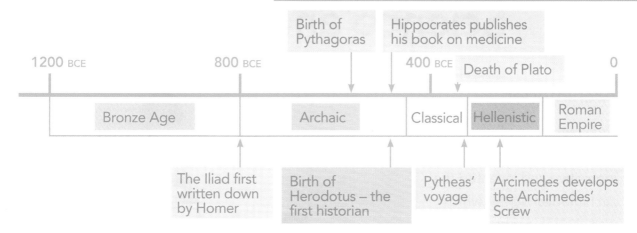

Birth of Pythagoras

Hippocrates publishes his book on medicine

Death of Plato

1200 BCE   800 BCE   400 BCE   0

Bronze Age | Archaic | Classical | Hellenistic | Roman Empire

The Iliad first written down by Homer

Birth of Herodotus – the first historian

Pytheas' voyage

Arcimedes develops the Archimedes' Screw

didn't like the play or the acting, they often threw food – or even stones – at the actors on the stage!

Tragedy and comedy

The first plays were tragedies – serious plays with a moral based on the stories and myths of the Greek Gods. Aeschylus, Euripides and Sophocles each wrote many plays, and they are the only authors of Greek tragedies whose plays survive today. Later, writers like Aristophanes wrote comedies, based on real life. They were often very rude about the people and politicians of the time! Aristophanes was Athenian, and many of his plays protested against the war with Sparta.

Masks like these were used by the actors in the theatre

Think about it!

1. How do you think the people in the back rows of the theatre saw and heard the play?
2. Why do you think Greek tragedies were based on myths and stories about the gods? What does this tell us about the significance of religion *and* theatre to the Ancient Greeks?

Let's do it!

1. Research each of the famous Ancient Greeks in this unit. Find out what each of them was famous for. You might like to use a table like this one:

Famous Greek	*Why were they famous?*

2. You will need to add to this table in Units 7.2 and 7.3.

Archimedes

Archimedes was born in 287 BCE. He was very inquisitive and invented the Archimedes' Screw, which was used to supply water to the land. It is still the basis of many devices used today to raise water from a lower level to a higher one. He is said to have invented a 'death ray' weapon, using a powerful mirror to focus the sun's rays on wooden ships and setting them on fire! Perhaps he is most famous for discovering 'Archimedes' principle', which explains why objects sink or float. Archimedes is supposed to have made

Archimedes' Screw, used to raise water from lower level to a higher level

this discovery when stepping into his bath. This caused him to exclaim 'Eureka!' ('I have it!') and run down the street naked!

Aristarchus of Samos

Aristarchus was a Greek astronomer, born around 310 BCE. He was the first person to realise that the sun was at the centre of the known universe, and that the earth and the planets revolved around the sun. He was told that he was stupid for not keeping the earth at the centre!

Socrates

Socrates was a philosopher who lived in the 3rd century BCE. He wrote nothing, but believed that the best way to discover truths, however unpleasant, was by discussion. He argued it was our duty to question all common beliefs. His arguments were so unsettling that he was condemned to death for corrupting the youth of Athens. He was forced to commit suicide by taking poison.

Medicine

Hippocrates

The Greeks were famous for their medical knowledge. They believed a healthy lifestyle would keep you well. Hippocrates was born on the island of Kos in 460 BCE and wrote many books – some of which were still being studied by doctors in Europe in 1700! He developed the theory of the four humours. These were liquids within the body – blood, phlegm, yellow bile and black bile. If you were ill, it was because these humours were out of balance. The Greeks thought that, to cure you, all a doctor had to do was restore the correct balance inside your body. New doctors today still take the Hippocratic Oath when they begin to practise medicine. They promise, among other things, to do no harm to their patients.

Illustration from a 1574 medical textbook, Germany, showing the four humours

Asclepions

Many Greeks believed illness was a punishment by the gods for not behaving correctly. To get well, you needed to visit an asclepion. This was a temple devoted to healing. They were named after Asclepius, the god of healing. At the asclepion, the sick person would make a sacrifice to Asclepius, and perhaps sleep there overnight. Often a model of the infected part of the body would be left at the asclepion as an offering.

Ruins of the Asclepion of Pergamum, Turkey

Think about it!

1. Do you think the Greeks were more advanced in science or medicine?
2. What might it be like to visit an asclepion? How would you feel? What would you see? What would you think? What would you do?

Let's do it!

1. Update your table from Unit 7.1, and add famous Ancient Greeks from Unit 7.2.

The Greeks were skilled mathematicians. By 500 BCE, they had developed their own number system:

Value	1	2	3	4	5	10	20	21	50	100	500	1000
Greek Herodianic Numeral	I	II	III	IIII	Γ	Δ	ΔΔ	ΔΔI	Γ͞	H	Γ͞H	X

Example:
4672 would be shown as : XXXXHHHHHHΓ͞ΔΔII

They were able to carry out complicated number activities using an abacus like this one:

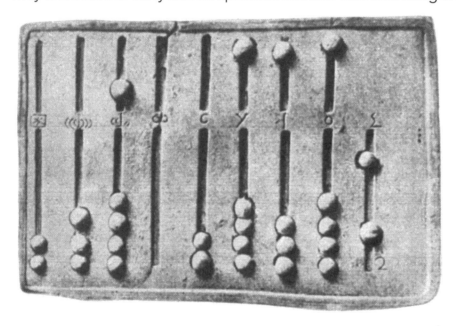

Modern replica of a Greek abacus, made of marble with either metal or pebble counters. The original dates from the 5th century BCE

Pythagoras

More than anything else the Greeks developed the idea of geometry. Pythagoras is regarded as the founder of geometry. He and his followers depended on logic to work out relations between numbers, whereas previously people had relied on intuition. Pythagoras is probably best known for his theory about right-angled triangles: 'In a right-angled triangle the square of the hypotenuse is equal to the sum of the squares of the two other sides.' Some historians now suggest that this idea was used by the Babylonians and Indians long before Pythagoras was born, saying that he was just the first to introduce this idea into Greek thinking. Pythagoras became convinced that the whole universe was based on numbers, and that the planets and stars moved according to mathematical equations. Pythagoras and his followers were the first to think in terms of odd, even and squared numbers.

Think about it!

1. Try doing some sums using the Greek number system. How easy is it to use?
2. How similar is the Greek abacus to one you might use in school today?
3. Add Pythagoras to the table you have made for famous Ancient Greeks (Unit 7.1).

Significance

Historian and history teacher Ian Dawson believes someone is significant if he or she:

- changed events during the time they lived
- improved lots of people's lives – or made them worse
- changed people's ideas
- had a long-lasting impact on their country or the world
- was a really good or very bad example to other people so to how to live or behave.

In this unit, you have been exploring lots of famous Ancient Greeks. You might want to add other Ancient Greeks you have come across, who are not mentioned in this unit. There are plenty more! For each of them, you now need to decide just how important they were at the time, and how significant they are to us today. Remember: it is possible to be very significant in Ancient Greek times and not that important today, or vice versa. You can either use Ian Dawson's criteria above, or you may have your own ideas about what makes people significant.

Let's do it!

1. One way to decide who is the most important Ancient Greek is to rank each one on a scale of 1 to 10, with 10 being most important. That way, you can develop an order of importance. Once you have done that, you might like to compare your list with others in your group and see if you agree.
2. Finally, hold a debate. Each of you argues for one person as the most famous Ancient Greek.

Around 500 BCE, the people of Athens invented the idea of democracy. This means that everyone can vote or take part in running the country or city. Today, many countries call themselves democracies, where everyone takes part in choosing the government by voting in elections. In fact, in some countries – like Australia – it is compulsory to vote and you get fined if you don't.

In most countries, everyone over the age of 18, male and female, can vote. However, it is just over 100 years since women have been able to vote in Britain. In Athens, only citizens could vote. That meant slaves could not vote, and some historians suggest there were nearly as many slaves as there were citizens in Athens. Women could not vote, either, so basically democracy in Athens meant male citizens meeting and deciding on laws and policies. You were called an idiot if you didn't take part in democracy!

Citizens of Athens meeting to make a new law

A fair trial?

Just like today, if you broke the law, a trial was held. This is a way to find out if you were innocent or guilty, and also to decide how to punish you (if you were found guilty). The Greeks were the first to introduce trial by jury, a system we still use today. Nowadays, in most trials 12 men or women are chosen at random to listen to the evidence and decide the verdict. The Greeks didn't use 12, they used up to 500, but you had to be a man aged over 30 to take part. A person's guilt was decided by a majority vote.

Socrates defends himself at his trial in 399 BCE. He was found guilty

Ostracism

If people thought someone was getting too powerful in the city-state, they could demand a vote for ostracism. Citizens were given a pot shard, a small piece of pottery, that they could write someone's name on. If enough people voted in this way, the person was then **banished** for 10 years. This meant they had to leave the city, and could not return. This system was designed to make sure that democracy worked. The equivalent today is the power to **impeach** a president or politician if they break the law.

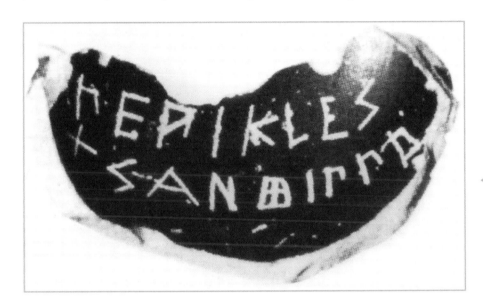

◀ Pot shard with the name of Pericles. It was used in c435 BCE in an attempt to get him banished for 10 years

Think about it!

1. Did everyone have a say in how Athens was run?
2. What happened to politicians who were unpopular?
3. Why do you think Greek boys were taught to speak well in public?

Let's do it!

1. How is the Government chosen in the country you live in? Is it similar to that in Athens?
2. Find out if all trials use juries to decide if someone is guilty.
3. 'The Greeks invented good government.' Do you agree?

Key words

banished

impeach

The Romans

The Romans were perhaps the first people to be **infatuated** with Greek styles and buildings. They copied Greek buildings, temples and statues, and even adopted many of the Greek gods as their own! And it was in Italy that some people in the 18th and 19th centuries came across Greek-style buildings.

Neo-Classical architecture

In the 18th century, ideas from the Classical world were all the rage. Rich people would copy Greek styles and build houses like the one below – Chiswick House in London, built for Lord Burlington. It became known as the Neo-Classical style ('Neo' = new; 'Classical' = the ancient world).

Statue of the Greek goddess Artemis. This is a Roman copy of a Greek original

At the time, rich people went on a 'Grand Tour' of Europe, including Greece and Rome, a trip that often lasted two or three years. They brought home statues, paintings and lots of 'new' ideas. Houses were rebuilt in the style of Greek temples, and gardens were filled with decorative buildings, waterways and bridges in the Neo-Classical style. Walls were covered with paintings and **tapestries** depicting Greek myths and heroes. Authors wrote books about Ancient Greece, and Greek was the number one language taught to boys. It even became fashionable to collect relics and artefacts from Ancient Greece and Rome. Some people set up private museums in their own homes to show off what they had brought home from their Grand Tour.

Chiswick House, built in the Neo-Classical style

Public buildings

It wasn't just homes that were built in the Neo-Classical style. The British Museum was built between 1825 and 1850, to house a growing collection of books and artefacts from across the classical world, including marble statues collected from the Parthenon by Lord Elgin. The Greek Government demanded that Britain returns the Parthenon Marbles to Greece because

Stock Exchange in Oslo, Norway, opened in 1828

they say it is where they belong. In Germany, the Brandenburg Gate, which was built 1787–1791, reflects the shape and size of a Greek temple. Both the Oslo Stock Exchange (opened in 1828) and Ireland's Parliament House (built in 1729) were built in similar ways. All these public buildings, built and owned by governments, used the Greek style of architecture to emphasise their importance. The British Museum, for example, was designed to show that Britain, like Ancient Greece, was strong and powerful and had a great empire. Architects still design and build in the Neo-Classical style today.

Think about it!

1. How similar are these houses and public buildings to Greek temples?
2. Why might governments want to copy Greek buildings?

Let's do it!

1. Research some of the buildings mentioned on this page. When were they built? Who designed them? Who paid for them? Are they still in use today?
2. Find out about the Grand Tour. Where did people go, and what did they do? What impact did it have on life in the 18th and 19th centuries?
3. Do you think the Parthenon Marbles should be returned to Greece? Research the arguments on both sides and explain your answer.

Key words

infatuated

tapestries

47

What *else* did the Greeks do for us?

There are many other Greek inventions that have helped to shape the world we live in. The Greeks built the first ever lighthouse, in Alexandria, in around 280 BCE. It was said to be 100 metres tall, and lit by a huge furnace at the top. It was one of the Seven Wonders of the Ancient World. Eventually it was destroyed by earthquakes. However, in 1997, French underwater archaeologists found some of it sunk in the harbour of Alexandria.

Illustration showing the Lighthouse of Alexandria – one of the Seven Wonders of the Ancient World

Map-making

Anaximander is said to have invented **cartography**, or map-making. He was born in 610 BCE in Ionia, which today is part of Turkey. It is claimed that he was the first man to publish a map of the world. Not surprisingly, large areas of the world were not included, as the Greeks didn't really know any of the world away from the Mediterranean Sea. Again, perhaps it is not a surprise that Greece, and especially Ionia, is drawn at the centre of the world!

What people today think Anaximander's map looked like

Other Greek inventions include the alarm clock; the anchor, to secure ships in the sea; and the watermill, for grinding wheat into flour. The second part of the Bible, the New Testament, was written in Greek. The Greeks also invented the crane to help with their building work. Therefore, it is clear that the Greeks have had a huge influence on modern society. No wonder many people regard them as the founders of the modern world!

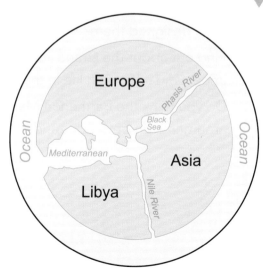

Think about it!

1. What would your life be like without maps, alarm clocks, cranes and lighthouses?
2. How accurate is Anaximander's map? How useful is it to us today? How useful was it to the Ancient Greeks?

Let's do it!

1. It is now time to answer this question: 'What did the Greeks do for us?' Throughout this book, there have been lots of examples to show how the Ancient Greeks have had a big influence on modern-day life. Go back through the whole book and make a list of as many as you can.
2. Once you have your list, sort it into two: 'Big impacts' and 'Not so big impacts'. This should help you decide priorities. Sort each list into a rank order, putting those with the biggest impact at the top of your list.
3. Discuss your lists with others in your group. Are their lists the same as yours?
4. Finally, make a presentation about the impact of Ancient Greeks on modern-day life. You need to decide *how big* an impact they have had, as well as which has had the *biggest* impact.

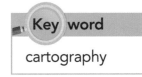

Key word

cartography

Skills grid

Unit	Skills
1	chronology and sense of period
2	similar and different, interpretations
3	using evidence to reach your own conclusion
4	presenting a researched piece of work
5	causation, similar and different
6	continuity and change
7	significance
8	reaching a reasoned judgment based on knowledge of Ancient Greece

Eat like a Greek

Most Greeks had a simple diet – lots of bread and olive oil. People ate a lot of fruit and fish. However, only the rich could afford to eat meat, except on very special occasions, when other people could too.

Breakfast

Breakfast was usually bread. It was probably quite hard, left over from the day before. Sometimes they ate a type of pancake made from flour, oil, milk and honey. In Athens, there were so many bakeries that nearly everybody bought their bread rather than baked it themselves.

Lunch

Lunch was another simple meal, and was more like a snack. Most people ate bread, cheese, salted fish, and fruit such as figs and olives.

Evening meal

Men and women would eat separately – the men would eat first! Eggs, fish, vegetables and cucumbers, cheese, bread, nuts and beans were all popular foods. Sometimes the men would have a symposium, or feast, where they would eat with lots of food. They might be entertained by musicians, dancers and acrobats, or hold poetry competitions. The men might even carry out some business, before the party got too noisy.

Bowl showing the importance of fish in the Greek diet

Do you think the Ancient Greeks had a healthy diet?

A Greek symposium, or feast for men only!

A healthy diet?

Today, many people in the world suffer from **obesity** – being overweight – and don't take enough exercise. Medical advice is to eat a 'Mediterranean-style diet'. Some doctors claim that eating a Mediterranean-style diet can extend your life by 15 years, because it leads to less cancer and a healthier heart, for example.

Let's do it!

1. Find out about the Mediterranean-style diet. What foods does it include? Why is the diet thought to be so much healthier than the way most people eat today?
2. How is this diet similar to the diet of the Ancient Greeks?
3. Does that mean the Ancient Greeks were healthier than we are today?
4. How similar is the food eaten by Ancient Greeks to the traditional diet where you live?

How healthily do you eat?

- Keep a food diary for a week. Record *everything* you eat and drink for a whole week. Be honest with yourself, and don't cheat! A table like this might be helpful:

	Monday	Tuesday	Wednesday	Thursday	Friday	Saturday	Sunday
Breakfast food							
Breakfast drinks							
Lunch food							
Lunch drinks							
Dinner food							
Dinner drinks							
Snacks							

- How does your diet compare to the diet of an Ancient Greek? Which foods do you eat more of? Which foods do you eat less of?
- Is your diet healthier than that of an Ancient Greek?
- Find out what Romans, Anglo-Saxons and Vikings ate. How similar were their diets to your diet and the Ancient Greeks' diet?
- Who ate the healthiest foods?

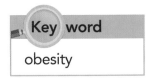

Key word

obesity

51

Film as history

Sense of period

One of the hardest things in history is to develop a 'sense of period'. What was it *really* like living in Ancient Greece? What could you see? Hear? Smell? Do? Film is really good for helping to develop a sense of period. You get to see and hear all the action, rather than relying on one written source or image.

Film as a source of information

Film can present a huge range of information very quickly, and many people use film as a source of evidence about a period. However, it is important to remember that film usually offers us just one interpretation of events, whereas history is very complicated. Perhaps the best way to use film is to see if the content matches up with what you already know. If the hero in the Boer War (1899–1902) is riding in a tank (invented in 1916), then we know something is wrong! Sometimes films provide misinformation. This is either because the producers have been lazy and not done their research, or because the facts get in the way of a good story! The film *The 300 Spartans*, released in 1962, tells the story of the Battle of Thermopylae in 480 BCE, during the Persian Wars. Lots of the story is fairly close to the history of the battle, but much is changed too. Can you tell the difference?

Still from the film The 300 Spartans, *released in 1962*

Think about it!

1. What are the advantages and disadvantages of using film in history lessons?

2. How can you tell if the producers of a film have done their history homework?

What can you tell about Ancient Greece from a film?

Films are meant to entertain. They are designed to make money, rather than stick to the historical facts. A film only gives us one interpretation of history, which is based on the facts the film-makers choose to use.

How useful is film to us in understanding life in Ancient Greece?

The Disney film *Hercules* was released in 1997. It claims to tell the story of Hercules, or Herakles as we know him, who we met in Unit 4.3. Herakles is forced to carry out 12 labours before he is forgiven for murdering his wife and children in a fit of madness. He is the son of Zeus, King of the gods, and has godlike powers that help him to complete his labours.

Let's do it!

1. Read the story of Herakles. It is one of the most famous Greek myths. What are the Twelve Labours he is asked to do? How does he manage to successfully complete them all? What does the story of Herakles add to our understanding of Ancient Greece?

2. How closely does the film *Hercules* stick to the story? Is it an accurate retelling of the myth? How is it similar, and how is it different?

3. Is there any part of *Hercules* that helps us to understand life in Ancient Greece?

Alexander was born in 356 BCE, and was the son of Philip II, King of Macedonia. Philip conquered Greece and united the country. When he was 13, Philip chose the famous Greek philosopher and scientist Aristotle to tutor him. He learned politics, philosophy, drama, poetry and science. In 336 BCE, Philip was killed by one of his bodyguards, and Alexander became King. He was immediately faced with lots of **rebellions**, but he defeated them all and remained in power. People didn't like the idea of being ruled by such a young man.

Roman mosaic, 1st century CE, from a house in Pompeii. It shows Alexander leading his army against the Persians

One day, Alexander was watching soldiers trying to train a wild horse. No one was able to calm the horse, put on a bridle and ride it. He noticed that it was scared of its own shadow, so he approached the horse from the other side and was quickly able to settle the horse down and even ride it. From then on, Alexander rode the horse wherever he went. Some people said he loved his horse Bucephalus more than he loved his family.

Alexander tames his horse Bucephalus

Alexander's empire

Over the next decade Alexander conquered country after country. Persia, Iran, Iraq, Egypt and even parts of India fell to him. He was also planning to conquer North Africa. It is said he rode over 18,000 kilometres with his army. Unusually for the time, he treated his soldiers very well, and paid them quickly (they earned lots of goods from all his victories). Therefore, they were very loyal to him, and followed him everywhere. By the time he died in 323 BCE, of a fever in Baghdad, Alexander ruled an empire that covered three continents.

He ran toward the horse and seized the bridle

The empire of Alexander the Great by 323 BCE, showing the sites and dates of battles

Alexander's legacy

Some historians suggest that Alexander was the greatest general who ever lived. He developed new methods of fighting and often defeated enemy armies that were much larger than his own. He spread Greek influence, language and culture over a huge area. He established the city of Alexandria in Egypt, which became both a centre of great learning and a major trading city in the Mediterranean region. He started the Hellenistic age of Greek history, which lasted until the Romans conquered the Greeks. When he died, his Empire **disintegrated** into separate states – there was no one else strong enough to hold it together.

Think about it!

1. Do you think the way Alexander is shown on the Roman mosaic is accurate?
2. What does the story of Alexander and the horse tell us about Alexander as a person?
3. How important was Alexander in spreading the ideas of Greece around the world?

Let's do it!

1. Find out about Alexander's wars. Where were they fought? Why was he so successful?
2. Do you think Alexander was the greatest Greek ever?

Key words

rebellions
disintegrated

Ancient Greek clothes were simple and lightweight, made from linen or wool. The best woollen cloth was expensive. Later, rich people could buy cotton and silk imported from India, although poorer people often spun and wove their own cloth and made their own clothes. Linen was made from flax imported from Egypt. Clothes couldn't be too heavy, as it was quite hot in summer. Pins or brooches were used to tie clothing. Fabrics were coloured using dye from plants. The most common colours to use were violet, green and grey, while materials were decorated in checks, wavy lines, stripes and flowered designs. Coloured clothing was always more expensive than undyed fabric.

Most people went barefoot, although leather sandals and sometimes boots were worn, especially by soldiers. Both women and men would wear straw hats to protect them from the sun. Men working outside would often simply wear a **loincloth** made from linen. Rich women would wear jewellery made from silver or gold. Their hair was often tied up on top of their head.

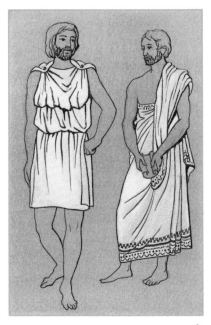

Man wearing a himation, or overgarment

Most women wore a simple chiton like this one, fastened around the waist with a belt

Think about it!

1. How well was Greek clothing adapted to the way of life and the climate of Ancient Greece?
2. Why were most people's clothes white?

Clothes through time

One of the units in the National Curriculum asks you to study a historical period after 1066. This is a good opportunity to look at changes right up to today. While studying Romans, Anglo-Saxons and Vikings, for instance, you will have looked at their clothes. How similar are these to clothes worn by the Ancient Greeks? Look carefully at the pictures of Tudor clothing on the next page.

What materials are the clothes made from? Are they tailored (or shaped) carefully, like clothes today, or are they loose, like those of Ancient Greece? What colours did they have?

Finally, have a close look at these people from the 1960s. How are their clothes different to Tudor clothes?

Outfits from the 1960s
▼

▲
Tudor clothing

Let's do it!

1. The best way to examine clothes is to think about these five headings:

   a What fabrics are they made from?

   b What colour are they?

   c Are they tailored or shaped in any way?

   d How expensive are they?

   e How suited are they to the weather where people live?

   Can you add any more headings to this list?

2. Look back over the history you have studied already. For each historical period, find out what people wore. Try to answer the five headings above. Collect pictures of typical clothes from the different times.

3. Present your findings with the heading, 'Clothes through the ages'. Try to discover how clothes have changed from Ancient Greek times to today.

4. Finally, decide which is your favourite period. Which clothes would you have liked to wear the most? Why?

Key word

loincloth

Glossary

Amphora: a Greek jar for transporting goods

Banished: kicked out of somewhere

Cartography: making maps

Chiton: simple woman's dress – could be long or short

Circumnavigating: sail all the way around a country or the world

Citadel: strongest part of a town, city or castle; best defended part

City-state: an independent country based on one city and the area immediately around it

Disintegrated: fell apart

DNA: helps scientists discover lots of genetic information

Draught: amount of ship that is below sea level – a shallow draught means a ship can sail nearer the shore

Fleece: wool from a sheep, cut off all in one piece

Historical narrative: story of what happened, based on historical evidence

Hoplites: Greek soldiers

Impeach: put on trial for doing something wrong, against the law

Infatuated: to really, really love, copy their ideas

Knots: speed of ships

Latitude: lines on a map that help you find out how far north or south of the equator you are

Loincloth: single piece of cloth, wrapped around the hips

Mosaics: pictures made up of lots of little coloured stones

Myth: story

Niche: small alcove, usually in a wall, for a statue of a god or goddess

Obesity: being very overweight

Obituary: report written when someone dies, telling people about their achievements

Orator: someone very good at speaking in public, at persuading people to support their ideas

Ottoman Empire: huge Muslim empire based in Constantinople from c15th until 1918

Parthenon: very famous temple in the middle of Athens

Phalanx: shield wall made by soldiers for protection in battle

Phoenicians: Ancient civilisation based around Lebanon; very successful trading nation around 1500 BCE

Rebellions: fights against your king or ruler

Renaissance: renewal or rebirth, period of history in Europe, c14th to c17th, where there were lots of changes

Residue: leftovers

Sacked: destroyed

Sacrificed: offered to the gods

Secluded: hidden away

Separate spheres: belief that life was split up into men's jobs and women's jobs

Shrines: special holy places

Soothsayer: a prophet (male or female) who it is thought can tell the future

Strait: narrow sea separating two pieces of land or islands

Tapestries: picture-carpets, made to hang on walls

Terraced: the slope turned into flat strips

Trireme: an Ancient Greek war ship with three sets of oars

Volunteered: done something because you wanted to, not because you were forced to do it

Index

World map

North Pole +

GREENLAND

ICELAND

NORWAY

UNITED
KINGDOM DENMA

IRELAND

GERMA

AUS

CR

FRANCE

ITA

CANADA

PORTUGAL SPAIN

UNITED STATES
OF AMERICA

MOROCCO

ALGERIA

MEXICO

CUBA

MAURITANIA MALI

NIGE

JAMAICA

SENEGAL

GUINEA

GUATEMALA

NICARAGUA

NIGERIA

COSTA RICA

VENEZUELA

GHANA

PANAMA

GUYANA

COLOMBIA

ATLANTIC
OCEAN

Equator

ECUADOR

GABON

PERU

BRAZIL

PACIFIC
OCEAN

BOLIVIA

NA

PARAGUAY

CHILE

URUGUAY

ARGENTINA

SOUTHERN O

South Pole +

ARCTIC OCEAN

RUSSIA

KAZAKHSTAN

MONGOLIA

RAINE

TURKEY

TURKMENISTAN

SYRIA

AFGHANISTAN

CHINA

JAPAN

PACIFIC
OCEAN

ISRAEL

IRAQ

IRAN

JORDAN

EGYPT

SAUDI
ARABIA

PAKISTAN

NEPAL

INDIA

MYANMAR

OMAN

SUDAN

ERITREA YEMEN

THAILAND

PHILIPPINES

VIETNAM

SOUTH
SUDAN

ETHIOPIA

SRI
LANKA

SOMALIA

MALAYSIA

KENYA

Equator

ATIC
C OF
GO

INDONESIA

PAPUA NEW
GUINEA

TANZANIA

INDIAN
OCEAN

SOLOMON
ISLANDS

BIA

MOZAMBIQUE

VANUATU

MADAGASCAR

NA

AUSTRALIA

NEW
ZEALAND

N

Acknowledgements

The publishers wish to thank the following for permission to reproduce images. Every effort has been made to trace copyright holders and to obtain their permission for the use of copyright materials. The publishers will gladly receive any information enabling them to rectify any error or omission at the first opportunity.

(t = top, c = centre, b = bottom, r = right, l = left)

p4 Greg Balfour Evans/Alamy Stock Photo; p7 © The Trustees of the British Museum. All rights reserved.; p8 N/A; p9t Red-figure Krater (ceramic), Greek, (4th century BC)/Museo Archeologico, Cefalu, Sicily, Italy/Bridgeman Images; p10 © The Trustees of the British Museum. All rights reserved.; p11t Egyptian scribe and Greek schoolboy (litho), English School, (20th century)/Private Collection / Look and Learn/Elgar Collection/Bridgeman Images; p11b Photo Oz/ Shutterstock; p12t Art Reserve/Alamy Stock Photo; p12b A Spartan whipping his slaves (gouache on paper), Jackson, Peter (1922-2003)/Private Collection /© Look and Learn/Bridgeman Images; p14b delcarmat/Shutterstock; p15 FAYEZ NURELDINE/Staff/Getty Images; p16t George Atsametakis/Alamy Stock Photo; p17 TonelloPhotography/Shutterstock; p18l World History Archive/Alamy Stock Photo; p18c Azoor Photo/Alamy Stock Photo; p18r Sword with gold hilt and bronze blade, from tomb 36, Necropolis of Zapher, Knossos, Greece / G. Dagli Orti /De Agostini Picture Library / Bridgeman Images; p20t airphoto.gr/Shutterstock; p20b KOSTAS TSEK/Shutterstock; p21 Zwiebackesser/Shutterstock; p22t elgreko/Shutterstock; p23 Votive stele depicting a sacrificial procession to Dionysus and Artemis. 4th century BC./ Tarker/Bridgeman Images; p24t Chronicle/Alamy Stock Photo; p24b rook76/Shutterstock; p25 The Picture Art Collection/Alamy Stock Photo; p26b Heritage Images/Contributor/Getty Images; p27 World History Archive/Alamy Stock Photo; p28t Lanmas/Alamy Stock Photo; p28b Leemage/Getty Images; p29 David Kilpatrick/Alamy Stock Photo; p30t Chris Hellier/Alamy Stock Photo; p30b Tamara Kulikova/Shutterstock; p32t Ivy Close Images/Alamy Stock Photo; p32b Ancient Art and Architecture/Alamy Stock Photo; p33 Public domain; p34 age fotostock/Alamy Stock Photo; p35t DEA/G. NIMATALLAH/Contributor/Getty Images; p35b DEA/G. DAGLI ORTI/Getty Images; p36 Ancient Art and Architecture/Alamy Stock Photo; p37 Heritage Image Partnership Ltd/Alamy Stock Photo; p38t Alvaro German Vilela/ Shutterstock; p38b WitR/Shutterstock; p39b M.Brodie/Alamy Stock Photo; p40 Universal Images Group North America LLC/Alamy Stock Photo; p41t INTERFOTO/Alamy Stock Photo; p41b Waj/Shutterstock; p42 INTERFOTO/Alamy Stock Photo; p44t Ivy Close Images/Alamy Stock Photo; p44b Chronicle/Alamy Stock Photo; p45 Granger Historical Picture Archive/Alamy Stock Photo; p46t Brittany Graham LA/Shutterstock; p46b Anthony Shaw Photography/Shutterstock; p47 Kiev.Victor/Shutterstock; p48t ClassicStock/Alamy Stock Photo; p50t DEA/G. NIMATALLAH/Contributor/Getty Images; p50b Ancient Athens - reconstruction of the Symposium (colour litho), Italian School/Private Collection/De Agostini Picture Library/Bridgeman Images; p52 AF archive/Alamy Stock Photo; p54t Araldo De Luca/Contributor/Getty Images; p54b Chronicle/Alamy Stock Photo; p56t De Agostini Picture Library/Getty Images; p56b Lebrecht Music & Arts/Alamy Stock Photo; p57l Walker Art Library/Alamy Stock Photo; p57r pbpgalleries/Alamy Stock Photo.

We are grateful to the following for permission to reproduce copyright material:

An extract on page 4 adapted from 'Jason and the Golden Fleece' in *Usborne Greek Myths* by Heather Amery and Linda Edwards, copyright © 2000 Usborne Publishing Ltd. Reproduced by permission of Usborne Publishing, 83-85 Saffron Hill, London EC1N 8RT, UK. www.usborne.com.